PLAN:

JACK'S HOUSE

PROPOSED: Three story house and barn

SCALE: ·25 cm = 1m

SIGNATURE

Jack

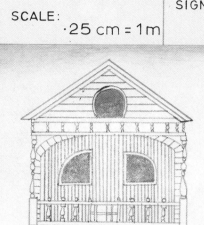

FRONT ELEVATION

E

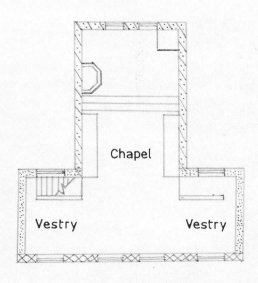

SECOND FLOOR

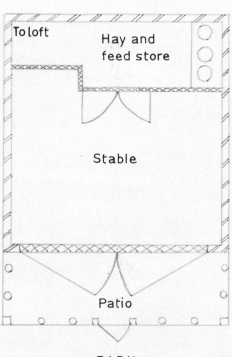

To loft

Hay and feed store

Stable

Patio

BARN

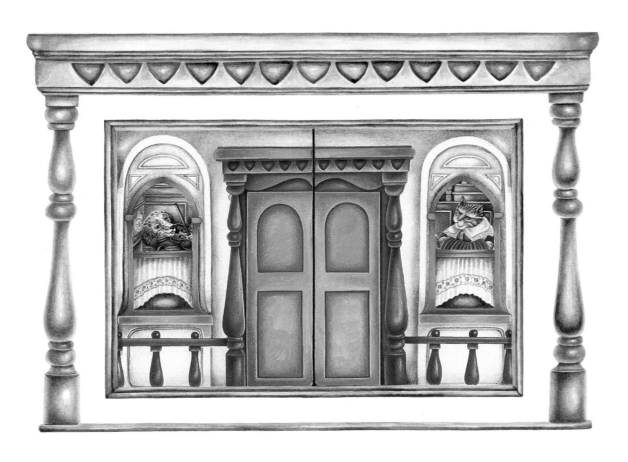

THE

HOUSE THAT

LIZ

THE

JACK BUILT

ILL   Henry Holt and Company · New York

For
Emma
and
Maysie

Illustrations copyright © 1987 by Liz Underhill
All rights reserved, including the right to reproduce
this book or portions thereof in any form.
Published in the United States by
Henry Holt and Company, Inc., 521 Fifth Avenue,
New York, New York 10175.
Originally published in Great Britain
by Methuen Children's Books Ltd.

Library of Congress Cataloging-in-Publication Data is available.
Library of Congress Catalog Card Number: 86-26999
ISBN: 0-8050-0339-8

First American Edition

Printed in Great Britain
1 3 5 7 9 10 8 6 4 2

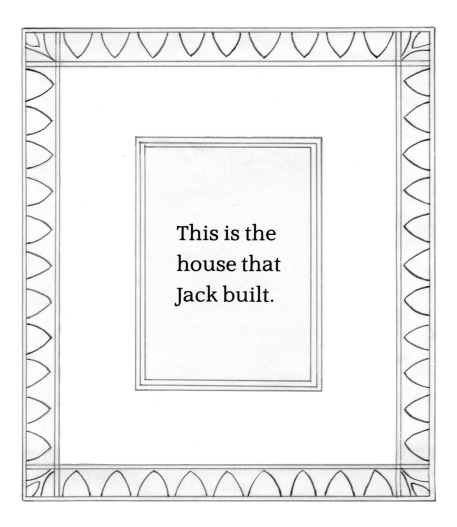

This is the
house that
Jack built.

THIS IS THE HOUSE
THAT JACK BUILT

This is the
malt,
That lay in the
house
That Jack
built.

This is the rat,
That ate the malt
That lay in the house
That Jack built.

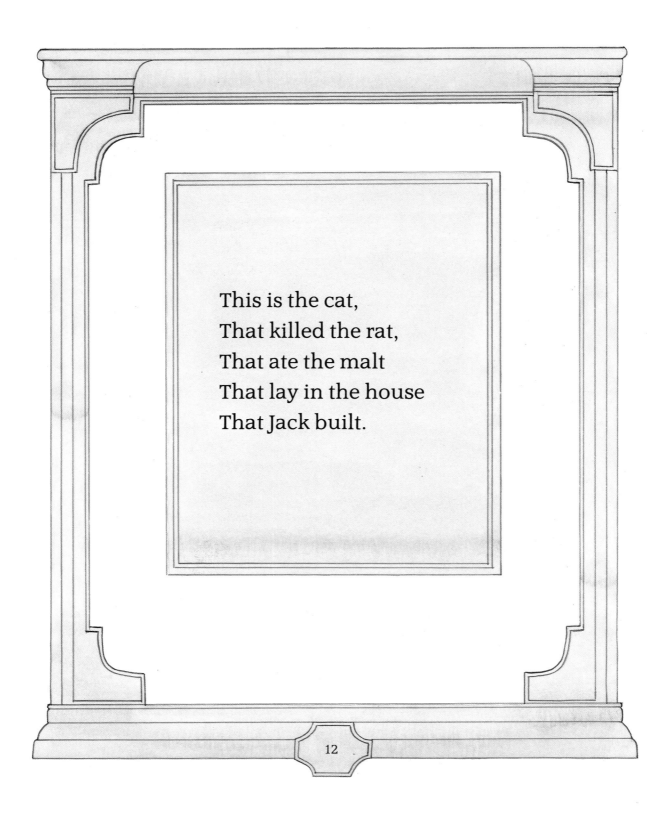

This is the cat,
That killed the rat,
That ate the malt
That lay in the house
That Jack built.

This is the dog,
That worried the cat,
That killed the rat,
That ate the malt
That lay in the house
That Jack built.

This is the cow w

That tossed the
        dog,
That worried the
        cat,
That killed the
        rat,

crumpled horn,

That ate the malt
That lay in the
house
That Jack built.

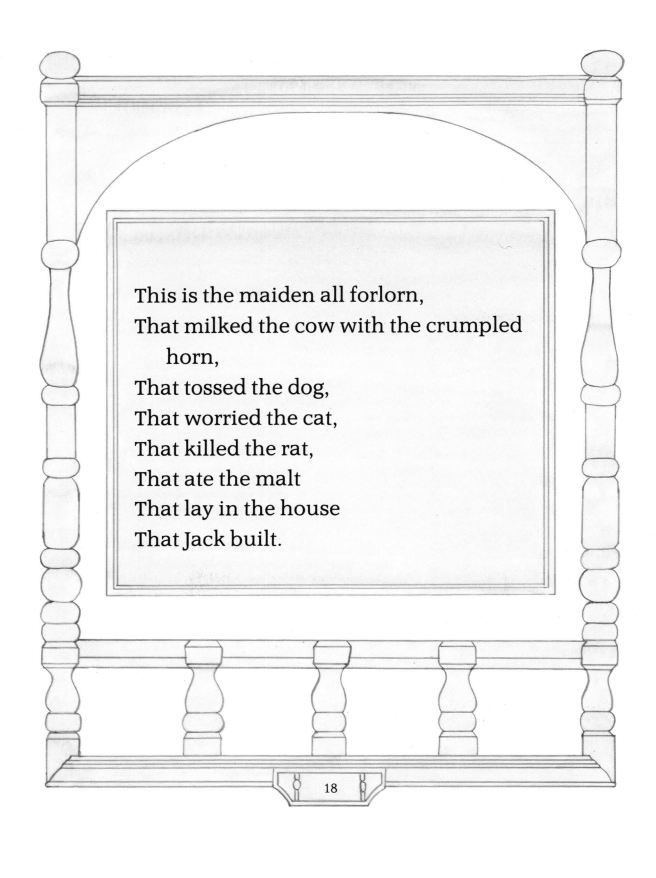

This is the maiden all forlorn,
That milked the cow with the crumpled
    horn,
That tossed the dog,
That worried the cat,
That killed the rat,
That ate the malt
That lay in the house
That Jack built.

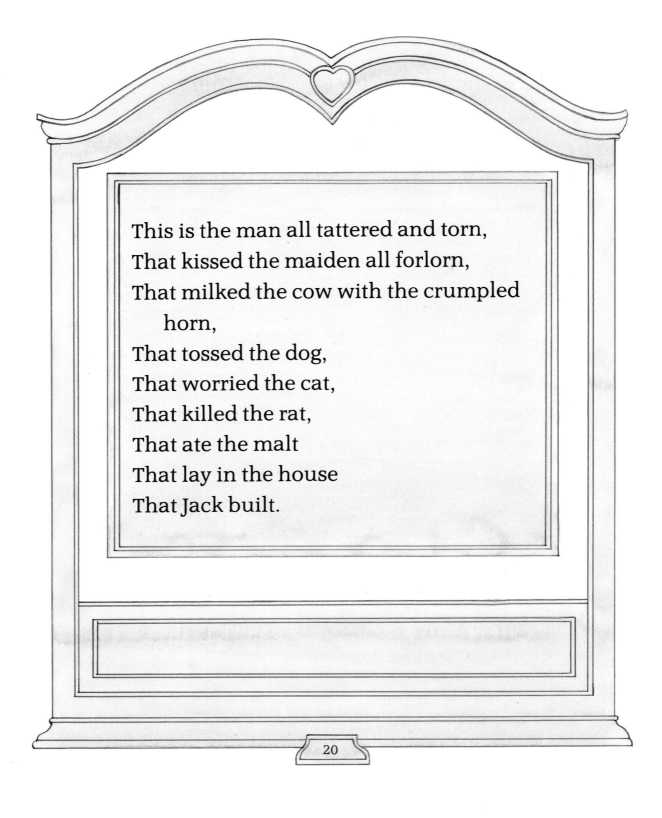

This is the man all tattered and torn,
That kissed the maiden all forlorn,
That milked the cow with the crumpled
     horn,
That tossed the dog,
That worried the cat,
That killed the rat,
That ate the malt
That lay in the house
That Jack built.

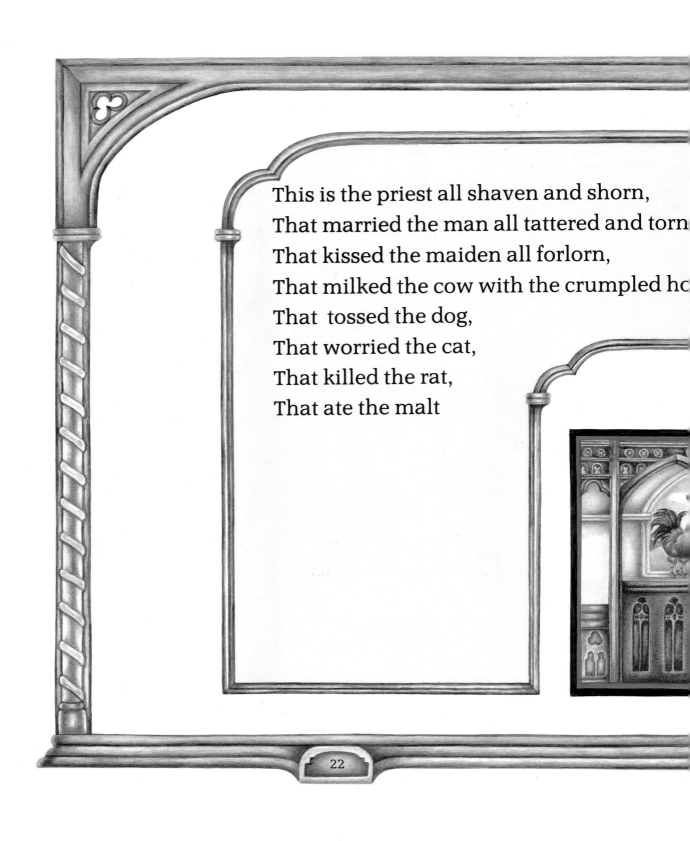

This is the priest all shaven and shorn,
That married the man all tattered and torn,
That kissed the maiden all forlorn,
That milked the cow with the crumpled horn,
That tossed the dog,
That worried the cat,
That killed the rat,
That ate the malt

That lay in the house
That Jack built.

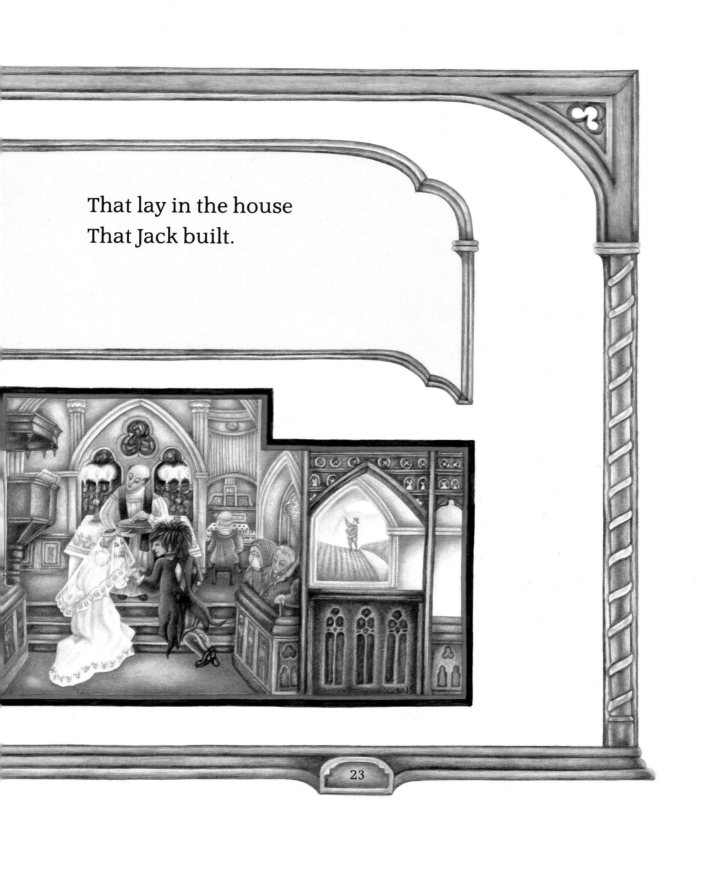

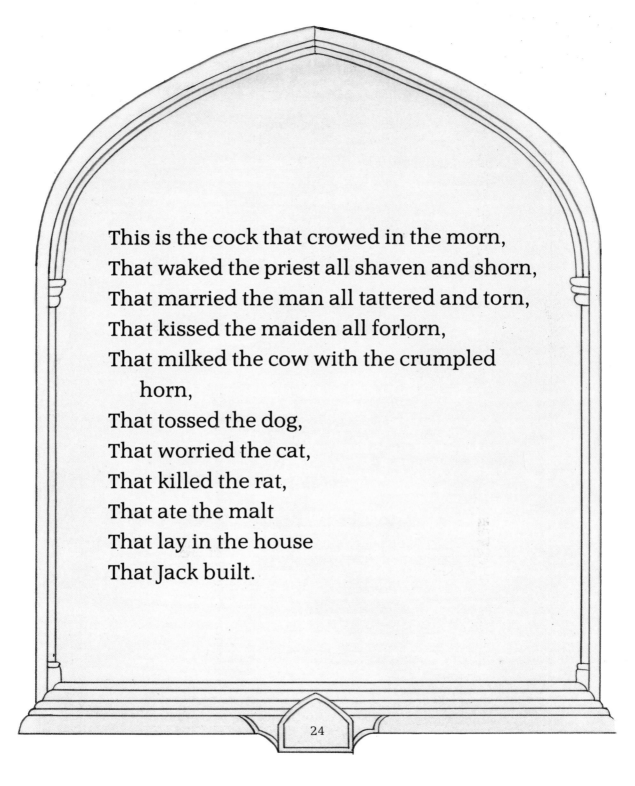

This is the cock that crowed in the morn,
That waked the priest all shaven and shorn,
That married the man all tattered and torn,
That kissed the maiden all forlorn,
That milked the cow with the crumpled
     horn,
That tossed the dog,
That worried the cat,
That killed the rat,
That ate the malt
That lay in the house
That Jack built.

This is the farmer sowing his corn,
That kept the cock that crowed in the morn,
That waked the priest all shaven and shorn,
That married the man all tattered and torn,
That kissed the maiden all forlorn,
That milked the cow with the crumpled
    horn,
That tossed the dog,
That worried the cat,
That killed the rat,
That ate the malt
That lay in the house
That Jack built.

27

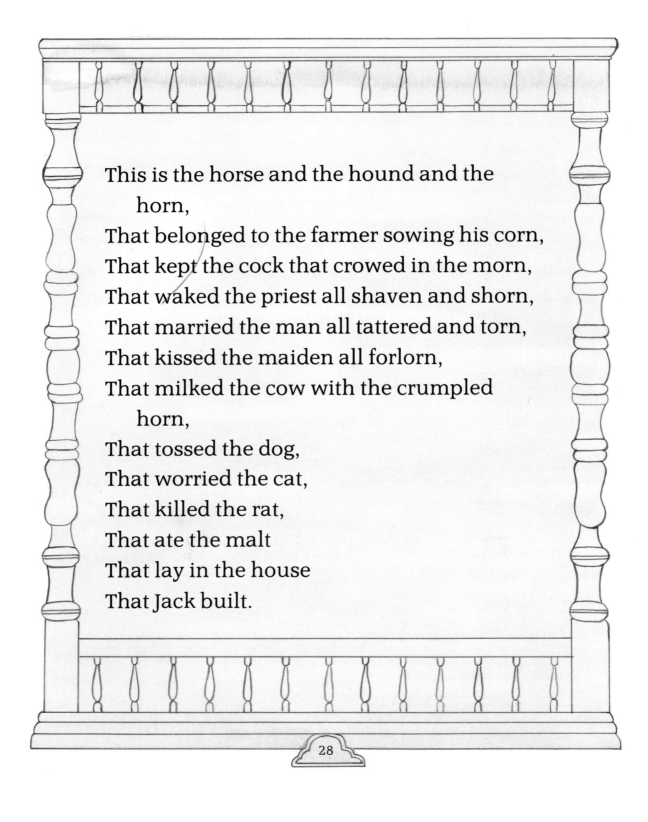

This is the horse and the hound and the
   horn,
That belonged to the farmer sowing his corn,
That kept the cock that crowed in the morn,
That waked the priest all shaven and shorn,
That married the man all tattered and torn,
That kissed the maiden all forlorn,
That milked the cow with the crumpled
   horn,
That tossed the dog,
That worried the cat,
That killed the rat,
That ate the malt
That lay in the house
That Jack built.

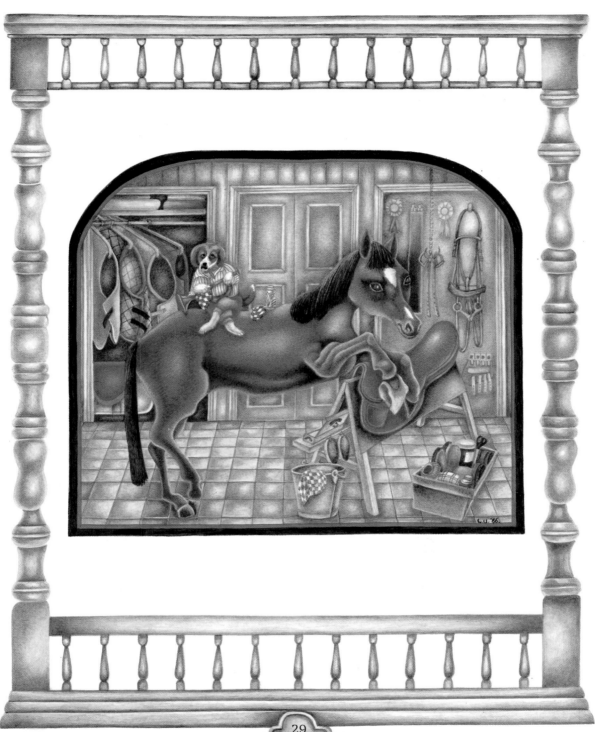

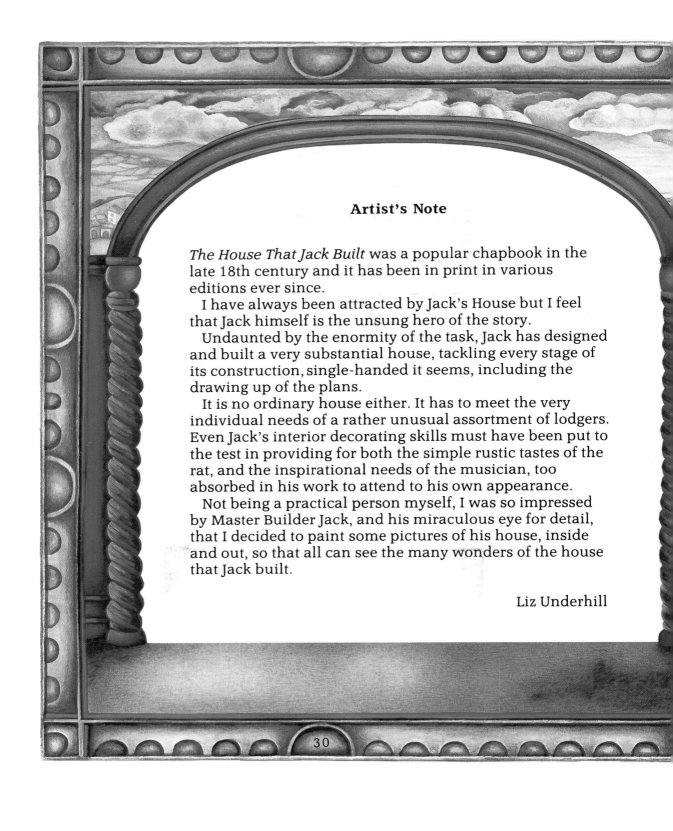

Artist's Note

The House That Jack Built was a popular chapbook in the late 18th century and it has been in print in various editions ever since.

I have always been attracted by Jack's House but I feel that Jack himself is the unsung hero of the story.

Undaunted by the enormity of the task, Jack has designed and built a very substantial house, tackling every stage of its construction, single-handed it seems, including the drawing up of the plans.

It is no ordinary house either. It has to meet the very individual needs of a rather unusual assortment of lodgers. Even Jack's interior decorating skills must have been put to the test in providing for both the simple rustic tastes of the rat, and the inspirational needs of the musician, too absorbed in his work to attend to his own appearance.

Not being a practical person myself, I was so impressed by Master Builder Jack, and his miraculous eye for detail, that I decided to paint some pictures of his house, inside and out, so that all can see the many wonders of the house that Jack built.

Liz Underhill

DATE DUE			
DEC 13 '89	MAR 0 5 2001		
DEC 20 '89			
APR 11 91			
FEB. 17 1992			
JUN 20 1992			
MAR 9 1993			
DEC 21 1993			
MAY 11 1994			
NOV 07 1994			
JAN 15 '96			

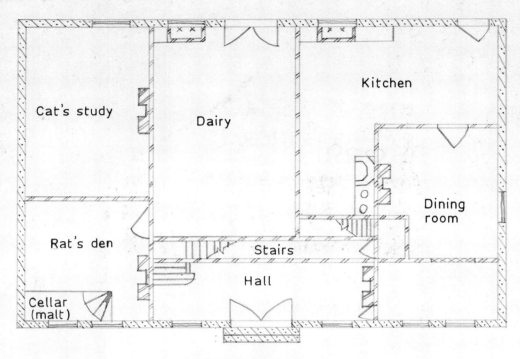

GROUND FLOOR

W ←

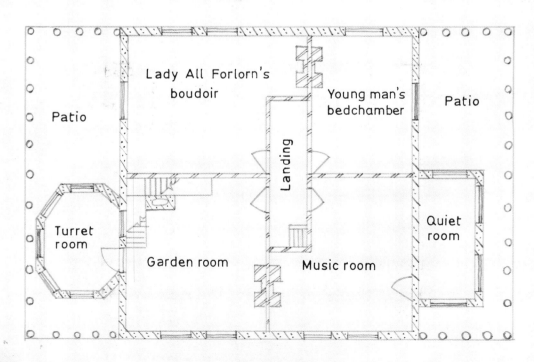

FIRST FLOOR